BARACK

By Jonah Winter   Illustrated by AG Ford

Collins
Katherine Tegen Books
An Imprint of HarperCollins*Publishers*

Collins is an imprint of HarperCollins Publishers.

Barack

Text copyright © 2008 by Jonah Winter

Illustrations copyright © 2008 by AG Ford

Printed in the U.S.A.

Library of Congress Cataloging-in-Publication Data is available.

ISBN 978-0-06-170392-8 (trade bdg.) — ISBN 978-0-06-170393-5 (lib. bdg.)

Typography by Rachel Zegar

1 2 3 4 5 6 7 8 9 10

First Edition

Looking back, it's hard to believe how far he has come, the man whose name the world now knows—BARACK OBAMA. This is a journey that began in many places.

It began in Kansas, home of Barack's mother.

It began in Africa, home of Barack's father.

It began in Hawaii one moonlit night, the night Barack was born.

Sometimes it was a sad journey. When Barack was just a toddler, his father moved far away.

Sometimes it was an enchanted journey. When Barack was only six years old, his mother brought him to Indonesia to live with her new husband.

For young Barack, Indonesia was a most exotic land. His stepfather kept an ape as a pet, and two crocodiles.

But it wasn't all wonderful in Indonesia. There was poverty unlike anything Barack's young eyes had ever seen.

And sometimes Barack felt very out of place. *Who am I?* he wondered, surrounded by his Indonesian classmates. He looked different from them. He spoke a different language. His birthplace was thousands of miles away. *Where do I belong?*

These were the questions Barack would ask again and again on this most unusual journey. But when the journey brought him back to Hawaii, alone, to attend an American school . . .

. . . the place where he belonged was with his loving grandparents,

who took good care of him until and after the thankful day
his mother returned to Hawaii with his new half sister, Maya,
only to go back to Indonesia, taking Maya with her.

Oh, sometimes it was a confusing journey. When Barack was only ten years old, his father just showed up one day, a total stranger.

Who was this man? Barack would wonder through the years, for this was the only time he ever saw his father, who had long since moved back to Africa.

And when his father packed his bags to leave again,
Barack could not stop imagining what his father's homeland,
Kenya, must be like.

On the other side of the world, there were half brothers,
half sisters, aunts, uncles. They wore different clothes. They
spoke a different language. And yet—they were his family.

Where do I belong? the voice inside his head kept asking. In school he had friends of all different backgrounds: African American, Caucasian, Hawaiian. He belonged with them all, but still . . .

Barack's mother was Caucasian. His father was African. So what did that make Barack? For Caucasians, it simply made him "black." For some African Americans, though, it made him *less* African American. *Who am I?*

Oh, but this was a journey on which Barack would find out exactly *who he was*—from his college days, when he learned how much he could move people just with the power of his words, in a speech . . .

. . . to his early days in Chicago, where his job was helping poor people help themselves, and helping them for very little pay. Some people thought he was too young, too privileged to ever understand their poverty.

Sometimes it was a lonely journey. *What am I doing here?* he often wondered, with the cold Chicago wind in his face, slowing him down, pushing him back. But he didn't give up.

For somehow his journey had led him to Trinity Church, surrounded by the people from his neighborhood, including many he had helped. And there, swept up in the waves of their singing, with tears on his cheeks, he knew why he was there. He knew who he was, and he knew where he belonged.

He was there in Chicago because he cared about these people.
They were his family. People in Kenya were his family. Indonesians
were his family.

And no matter where he was, the world was his home.

And who he was could be summed up in one word: lovable.

When you learn to love yourself, you make it easier for others to love you. That is what happened to Barack, who started climbing a ladder of popularity that led him to a seat in the Illinois State Senate,

and then up farther to the U.S. Senate.

He arrived here during a dark time in American history. All across America, people were losing their jobs, losing their houses, losing their sense of hope.

Many people were tired of a war that had gone on too long. They were tired of fighting with their neighbors over politics. They were just tired.

In an earlier age, there had been hope. There had been a man named Martin Luther King Jr. who had spoken with passion of his hope for better days. He had said, "*I have a dream that my four little children will one day live in a nation where they will not be judged by the color of their skin but by the content of their character.*"

And on the horizon, at the dawn of a new age, there appeared a man who would be the embodiment of King's dream—a presidential candidate whose very being was a bridge that joined nations.

Here was a man who spoke of "hope" and "change," whose strong words lifted up the downhearted people and made them believe that the world was not beyond repair.

Here was a man whose journey had brought him to cheering rallies all around America, including one in Birmingham, Alabama.

Birmingham was a place where policemen had once turned fire hoses on African Americans, who for many years were made to sit at the back of the bus, drink from separate drinking fountains, watch as their churches were burned to the ground, and here, *right here* . . .

Author's Note

BARACK OBAMA was born on August 4, 1961, in Honolulu, Hawaii. In the summer of 2008, as a Democrat, he became the first African American to become the presidential nominee for a major political party. (At the time this book went to press, the presidential election had not yet taken place.) Much could be said about how Barack rose to such importance by the young age of forty-six—about his racial background, about the influence of his mother, whose life's work involved helping people less fortunate than herself. In his autobiography, *Dreams from My Father*, Barack goes into great detail about all the things that shaped him.

But a person is larger than the sum of his parts, and Barack's history-making presidential candidacy was largely due to the quality of his character—and not simply to the color of his skin or to whom his parents were. Barack attracted a huge cross-section of Americans by calling out for a new unity—unity among people of all different colors, religions, and political viewpoints. As a community organizer in Chicago, Barack displayed a remarkable ability to get huge numbers of people working together to help their communities. And that's exactly what he did in his presidential campaign. All across America, people of many walks of life banded together to help him get nominated. They campaigned door-to-door. They made phone calls. They made donations, breaking new records. Rarely had an American presidential candidate generated such enthusiasm.

Many people have been inspired by Barack and his belief that we can overcome our differences and difficulties and achieve "a more perfect union." He spelled out his plan for a better America in his book *The Audacity of Hope.* This is the message with which Barack Obama achieved greatness.

. . . this great man spoke in a beautiful voice about his own dream of bringing people together, overcoming our differences, not just in America, but around the whole world.

Here, *right here*, in this country with its history of slavery and racism, an African American named Barack Obama rose to unimaginable heights because he refused to let other people tell him *who he was*, because again, once again, his journey was just beginning.

Author's Note

BARACK OBAMA was born on August 4, 1961, in Honolulu, Hawaii. In the summer of 2008, as a Democrat, he became the first African American to become the presidential nominee for a major political party. (At the time this book went to press, the presidential election had not yet taken place.) Much could be said about how Barack rose to such importance by the young age of forty-six—about his racial background, about the influence of his mother, whose life's work involved helping people less fortunate than herself. In his autobiography, *Dreams from My Father*, Barack goes into great detail about all the things that shaped him.

But a person is larger than the sum of his parts, and Barack's history-making presidential candidacy was largely due to the quality of his character—and not simply to the color of his skin or to whom his parents were. Barack attracted a huge cross-section of Americans by calling out for a new unity—unity among people of all different colors, religions, and political viewpoints. As a community organizer in Chicago, Barack displayed a remarkable ability to get huge numbers of people working together to help their communities. And that's exactly what he did in his presidential campaign. All across America, people of many walks of life banded together to help him get nominated. They campaigned door-to-door. They made phone calls. They made donations, breaking new records. Rarely had an American presidential candidate generated such enthusiasm.

Many people have been inspired by Barack and his belief that we can overcome our differences and difficulties and achieve "a more perfect union." He spelled out his plan for a better America in his book *The Audacity of Hope*. This is the message with which Barack Obama achieved greatness.